"James Merrill once wrote, 'To be twenty and a poet is to be twenty. To be forty and a poet is to be a poet.' Sean McDowell's first book, Learning to Jump, established him as a poet of unusual maturity. Galileo's Spyglass builds impressively on this achievement. As with his poem on Kepler's snowflake, these are lyrics of exceptional beauty, carefully constructed, everywhere alert to what Robert Herrick memorably called 'Times-transhifting.'"

—Jonathan F. S. Post is the author of Elizabeth Bishop: A Very Short Introduction

"McDowell's title poem narrating Galileo's labors to perfect the lenses that 'magnified his vision twenty, thirty / times normal sight' and allow him to watch 'the endless, unfolding, comingling light,' is the controlling metaphor for McDowell's own honing a craft that allows him to appreciate the radiant significance inherent in quotidian experience. I am particularly taken with his several poems of loss that manifest what Tagore calls 'the joy that sits still with its tears on the open red lotus of pain.'"

—Raymond-Jean Frontain, author of Reclaiming the Sacred: The Bible in Gay and Lesbian Culture

"It's rare for the same person to write an endorsement for an author, but it shouldn't be. If you go to a favorite restaurant and get a new and lovely dish, don't you want to share the news, even if you've badgered your friends before? And that's how it is with this new book by Sean McDowell, full of tender and reluctant elegies for friends and family ('Too many / old friends gone, or gone away'), ruminations on the fragile existence of animals and birds. It's a book that stresses gratitude, celebration, and a deliberate tenacity to live this life as well as possible. In one poem, he calls his uncle's recipe for tomato gravy a 'gift, comfort and remedy.' So are these poems."

—Samuel Green, author of Disturbing the Light

"Sean McDowell's Galileo's Spyglass is a beautiful book with his delicate, dreamy watercolor paintings carefully scattered like leaves through the volume, deepening the meaning of adjacent poems.

Who knew so many colors could be present in small paintings, reduced to blacks, greys, and whites. Intellect, knowledge, craft, and heart are in this book. His poems make present the past. Some are subtly connected. The poem about Galileo making his 'spyglass' is followed by Sean imagining the thoughts of the housemaid looking out the window, standing behind the woman writing a letter in Vermeer's famous painting. There are many poems about personal loss, mourning and memorializing beloved friends who have passed yet remain very present in these poems. Sean McDowell's beautifully crafted poems have powerful endings that pack an emotional punch that make you want to return to them, again and again."

—Achsah Guibbory, Professor of English, Barnard College

"What does one see through *Galileo's Spyglass*? The collection reaches deep down inside as much as it looks out to the stars and moon—or magnifies the beauty of the tiniest grain of dust or snow. It tells us of all sorts of losses, the deaths of loved ones or of a bird on Election Day, discarded books, disappointments and broken ties, neglect, oblivion and fear. But it looks at them in the face. McDowell's voice never gives into self-complacency or self-pity; it is fueled by a genuine generosity that makes us commune with everything that breathes and lives, however close or remote, in time or in space. 'Gift, comfort, and remedy' are to be found in the simple gestures and objects of everyday life, in shared cooking and handiwork that thread those who do it together, or in the wind that sways the nearby trees. McDowell's ink runs free, working 'by trial,' and yet it is steadfast and true like the 'Carpenter's Square,' shaping powerful and playful poems that possess the precision of artisan work. Like St. Francis, he works miracles with the humblest tools that fall between his hands—because making is love. His paintbrush too translates into monochrome watercolors—all black and white— a world vibrant with color and sounds, light and shadows, inviting us further into transformative meditation."

—Anne-Marie Miller-Blaise, Professor of English
Literature and History, Université Sorbonne Nouvelle

Galileo's Spyglass

Also by Sean McDowell:

Poetry

>   *Learning to Jump*

Prose

>   *Metaphysical Shadows: The Persistence of Donne, Herbert, Vaughan, and Marvell in Contemporary Poetry*

GALILEO'S SPYGLASS

Poems by

Sean McDowell

RESOURCE *Publications* · Eugene, Oregon

GALILEO'S SPYGLASS

Copyright © 2025 Sean McDowell. All rights reserved. Except in the case of brief quotations embodied in critical articles and reviews, no part of this book may be used or reproduced in any manner whatsoever without prior written permission from the publisher. Write: Permissions, Wipf & Stock, 199 W. 8th Ave., Suite 3, Eugene, OR 97401.

Resource Publications
A Division of Wipf and Stock Publishers
199 W. 8th Ave., Suite 3
Eugene, OR 97401

www.wipfandstock.com

Library of Congress Cataloging-in-Publication Data is available.

Paperback ISBN: 979-8-3852-5796-6
Hardcover ISBN: 979-8-3852-5797-3
eBook ISBN: 979-8-3852-5798-0

For Andrea, Tessa, Kieran, and Jensen

and for my mother, Virginia Lofendo

Acknowledgements

Several poems in this collection first appeared, in earlier and sometimes slightly different forms, in the following publications: *The Madrona Project* ("Five Friends," "Tomato Gravy," and "Galileo's Spyglass"); *Scintilla* ("Easter Winged"); *Literary Matters* ("After Vermeer," also known as "The Woman Waiting on the Woman Writing a Letter"); *John Donne Journal: Studies in the Age of Donne* ("Alder Sounds"); and *The High Window* ("Cure for Loneliness," "Mold-O-Rama," "Circuit," and "Discards"). I am grateful to the editors of these publications for introducing these poems to the wider world.

Quite a few people nudged me forward in my writing this time. David Boness, fellow aficionado of the history and philosophy of science, persuaded me to write not one poem about Galileo et. al. but several. A conversation with Mary Canavan about a painting conjured what would become the St. Francis of Paola poems. After my last book, Theo Dorgan's advice that I had better get cracking on the next one played like a mantra in my head. Other thoughtful readers, especially Gary Stringer, Raymond-Jean Frontain, George Klawitter, Claude Summers, Achsah Guibbory, Jeanne Shami, Jonathan F. S. Post, Dayton Haskin, Maria Salenius, Brent Nelson, Jason Wirth, Meg Lota Brown, Anne-Marie Miller-Blaise, Noreen Weihe, Beth and Gib Rossing, Joe Lane and Martha Simpson, and Jerry and Kathy Willins, encouraged me in this work. Many thanks as well to Paula Meehan, Heather Dubrow, Greg Miller, Mark Strohschein, Gabriella Gutiérrez y Muhs, Kimberly Johnson, Edwin Weihe, Tony Curtis, and Sam and Sally Green for their suggestions and insights.

All the illustrations in this book are original monochrome watercolors. My thanks to Charles Evans and Gail Coffey for emboldening me to paint them through their painterly wisdom.

This book is for my wife Andrea and our three vibrant children Tessa, Kieran, and Jensen, who inspire me daily with their light and laughter, and for my mother Virginia Lofendo, for a lifetime of belief.

Contents

Alder Sounds	3
Steller's Jay	4
Galileo's Spyglass	7
The Woman Waiting on the Woman Writing a Letter	9
Tomato Gravy	10
A Midwest Summer	12
St. Francis and the Burning Coal	14
Song for a Junco	15
Cure for Loneliness	16
Easter Winged	17
Our Lady of the Driveway	20
Coral Oak	21
Kepler's Snowflake	23
Procrastination	26
The Studio	27
How Much	29
St. Francis and the Fishes	30
Daily Rounds	32
Carpenter's Square	34
Tempting the Undertow	36
Circuit	37
Five Friends	39
To Chloe on the Way to Inis Mór	40
A Walk Along the Corrib	42
Endings	44

Adagio	45
Blush	46
The Storm	49
Discards	52
To Kristin in a Late May Mood	53
Barn Burning	56
Death of an Ohioan	57
Back Through Snoqualmie Pass	59
Street Moment	60
The Squirrel	61
The Abscessed Lover	63
Fear	64
Glossopetrae	66
St. Francis and the Strait of Messina	68
Mold-O-Rama	71
An Anniversary	73
Fresh-Picked	74
Boiling Penne	75
Painting the Moon	77
Candle	80
Undo List	81
New Listing	83

Illustrations

Alder in Wind	2
Moonlit Night	6
Hydrangeas	13
Hen Pecking Grain	25
Five Friends	38
The Storm	48
Its Aftermath	51
Somewhere in Branches Above	55
Shark	65
The Field Museum	70
Galilean Moon	79
Stepping Away	84

Galileo's Spyglass

Alder Sounds

for Judith H. Anderson

Tallest of neighborhood trees, the alder hoists
its mainsail of leaves against a cloudless sky.
Of all the trees nearby it speaks
loudest the language of wave crests,
waterfalls, sluice rush, and applause.

I have come to see our fading garden,
a string of losses in my head, to catch
and hold late September sunshine.
But the alder keeps me sitting here to cleanse
my ears of dread with its deciduous song.

Miles away, my friend, you lay dying, your world
contracted to a room. Can you still feel
the pleasure of soft pages in your hands?
Or have the body's rages drowned the words
of poets you love but leave behind too soon?

Wildfires ravage mountainsides East of here,
a death as immense as a city bombed,
a green world gone, like the one you coaxed
so lovingly from Spenser with a voice
I will remember as long as I draw breath.

Tomorrow winds will flood my street with smoke.
So I have come outside to hear the alder,
a glass of whiskey in my hand, before
the air turns toxic, before the leaves
fall silent—to listen while I can.

Steller's Jay

for Kimberly Johnson

Crested, arrogant, in-your-face,
yet bone-locked to the landscape in
a way few of us will ever be,

you flash-bulb my afternoon with
a surfer's swoop and glide and light
on the greenhouse gutter like a propane flame.

Cowled in midnight, clothed in deep dusk,
with incandescent stripes, your size
and full-throated *shaak-shaak-shaak* are

the terror of towhees and chickadees.
Yet today you eye the handfuls
of mixed nuts I left in a bowl

for a squirrel still nursing.
You coast in and beak an almond.
You'd swallow it whole if you could.

But I know your secret: you feed
a mate nesting in evergreen,
out-of-sight. Is this one for her?

Jay, jay, irrepressible jay,
you are a piece of the night sky
lit by a full moon. When you dart off

in a fluttering burst of blue,
you empty the yard of starlight.
Can none of us claim you for long?

Galileo's Spyglass

for David Boness

The Dutch built one first, crude little wonder,
two spectacle lenses, one convex, the other
concave stoppering both ends of an organ pipe.

And yet the two together could pluck
a galley in full sail from the horizon
and lift it close as if with giant hands.

From the moment he heard the sensation
it caused, he knew he could build one better.
In one day he had his own. Another

the next month, three times better.
Yet he reached farther, learned to work faster,
learned the craft of cutting a perfect disk

from the finest (and dearest) Venetian glass,
how to plane the edges smooth with iron,
how to hold it without slicing his skin.

Greek pitch smelled volcanic as he affixed
a working handle. He sprinkled a coarse mix
of Tripoli powder on a cannon ball

and rubbed in place a widening dimple.
The grit and grind sounded like sand underfoot
or like scraping caked ash and soot

from a fire-blackened flue. Soon glass gave way.
The curvature deepened. The disk became
an eyepiece no one yet could see through.

Now a vigorous buffing with fulled wool
and more powder, this time as fine as flour.
The murk dissipated like salt in water,

lens as clear as air. He worked by trial
and error in his making. He used a bowl
for convex lenses, grinding from the edges in,

tried all sorts of different combinations
and focal lengths galore. His discards,
propped and piled on tables and shelves, littered

his workshop like the plucked eyes of Argus.
Yet all his laboring and all his expense
magnified his vision twenty, thirty

times normal sight—a distance beyond any
earthly use. Merchants thought he was crazy.
His best work was useless on land or sea.

But he saw more. He sought the sky—and gasped
when he slid his spyglass into focus:
Mountains on the moon, Belt of Orion

filled with stars where stars were never seen.
He watched all through the cold, cloudless night
the endless, unfolding, comingling light.

The Woman Waiting on the Woman Writing a Letter

after Vermeer

All she wants to know is the bustling
market outside the window, watery
through stained glass and morning light.
Horses clop along the Langendyck,
stall keepers shout indistinctly,
the cries of gulls waver in and out.
The warp and weft of bodies in motion
on market day.
                  She half-listens
to the scritching of her mistress's quill,
secret words of love on precious paper.
She must wait for those words to dry,
the letter-locking, the hand-off to the boy
for delivery. Her ankles ache from standing,
from hours awake, her knees bent slightly
to forestall lightheadedness. Washing,
scullery work, the ongoing war
with dust throughout the day will trap
her indoors until late.
                        Yet while she waits
she's free to look, free to wonder,
free to wander in idle imaginings,
free to dream of life beyond these walls,
the red-roofed houses and church spires,
the avenues and canals, to where concerns
of men and demanding mistresses
concede to widening countryside
and all that might happen there.

Tomato Gravy

Always clever with a cleaver,
he crushed three garlic cloves beneath
its ricasso. Their inner peels
burst and slipped free as easily
as rice paper. He minced away,
rapid pecking of steel on wood,
then scraped the mincings into a pot
of stewed tomatoes he stewed again
with cracked peppercorns, pinches of salt,
diced bell peppers and onions so
pungent off the board they stung his eyes.

A blue gas flame whispered against
the copper bottom. Drop biscuits
browned in the oven. The mixture
burbled to a boil. As onions
faded and peppers lightened,
the kitchen steeped in lingering
aromas. A pat of butter
slid and pooled across a small
skillet. The flour he added made
a roux he stirred in slowly on
lowered heat to avoid burning.

Neither sauce nor stew but something
in between, it thickened into gravy
he ladled over halves of biscuits
and served with eggs and sausage,
bacon and berries, on a platter
too large for a normal person

but just right for a teenage boy
whose voice had yet to reach his height.
He dished himself one too, and we
tucked in, our knives and forks alive,
window fogged and beaded with steam.

My uncle perfected this dish
in the early 1960s
to warm weary servicemen in
from the bite and blow of Alaskan
cold on night-shrouded winter mornings.
It came to me, now comes to you,
as gift, comfort, and remedy.

A Midwest Summer

Through gaps between hydrangeas
like gun placements on the hill,
we tumbled down the slope,
head over heels in stuntmen rolls.

Our grunts and groans were hyperbolic
as we fell. Sprawled and panting,
we lay and stared at clouds forming
mountains. So much laughter then.

We climbed back up to roll back down,
steering clear of the duck pond's drain pipe
and its thick delta of mud. Outdoors
for hours as doves cooed, and cicadas

throbbed in oak trees, and bumblebees
buzzed globes of white flowers. Our skin
itched and smelled of grass. So passed
clockless afternoons, measured

in shifting patterns of leaf shadow
until the orange sunset glow
beyond the houses and treetops west
released the hill to bluing shade.

Mosquitos then, flecks of ash against
a dimming sky, their wings a dentist's
drill bit whine, their bites pinpricks
on our slapped forearms, necks, and knees.

Lightning bugs winked slow flashes
where darkness bloomed deepest. The stiff
spring of the old screen door yawned taut
and thwanged the door shut behind us.

St. Francis and the Burning Coal

Legend has it that when the boy from Paola,
like his namesake, the stigmata-ed friend
of animals, outpiety-ed the priests,

he sought refuge in a cave. Truffles,
borage, and chicory sustained him. He knew all
the spiders by name. Wolves stopped to lick his hands.

Sackclothed, he knelt beside a brazier
to soothe his spirit. Flames rolled and flared. Wood
pops flushed flocks of sparks. *Anything can happen.*

He reached in and scooped a coal from animate ash.
It glowed and crackled and shimmered, as warm
as a mother's breast on his unburnt palm.

Song for a Junco
Election Day, 2024

Quick little flash of black, brown, and grey
    it darts and ducks as it flies
from cedar limb to fence post, railing
    to feeder, where it dives and
pecks seed spillage with the urgency
    of an airlift under fire.
Some ghost of movement always spooks it
    into chattering flight and
it's off again to some safe elsewhere.
    How many times have I heard
it sing unseen its soprano bursts
    of *rit-tee-tee-tee-ta-tee*
somewhere among the leaves. But no more.
    This morning, like an arrow,
it struck a clear sheet of plexiglass
    meant to shield the porch from rain,
that one thump a shattering beneath
    its clean feathers. Now it lies
light and lifeless as a shuttlecock,
    soft as a whisper of mist
in the silence that replaces song.

Cure for Loneliness

When you feel as if you're forgotten,
take this cure with sad songs and red wine:
nine long walks along a storm-tossed shore,

nine missed sunrises, nine falling stars,
nine drams of whisky, nine drunken prayers,
and nine candles left to gutter out.

But never consult her photograph,
the one with sun and wind on her face,
lest all *your* forgetting go to waste.

Easter Winged

1

Their beaks were the pale orange
of summer squash, their plumage
as white as Easter lilies.
They shoveled water onto
their backs with backward head jerks,
fluffed to let it seep in,
and shrugged their wings, shuddering
like old men huddled against cold.
How they delighted in turning
about in their concrete pond,
idly paddling along.
How their clucks percolated
whenever they heard her voice,
these two Pekin ducks, orphaned
before they sprouted feathers.
What kept them penned there beside
the forked oak, when anyone,
even a small boy, could step over
the spindly wire encircling
the pond, the waist-high shed where
they slept on straw, the small patch
of grass they trampled to mud?
Her voice, yes. The way she sang
to them sometimes on bright days,
the canned sweet corn she brought them,
the slugs she gave them as treats,
the torn lettuce she tipped into
a water bowl, the leaves then
slippery enough to swallow.

Call it habit. Call it trust.
They preferred nowhere else,
and each morning they clamored
about her shins like children.

2

That Easter morning when nothing
seemed to rise, darkness hushed
the bedroom. The pocket door
shunted open, scrape of wood
on wood, and in the doorway
my grandmother's silhouette
beckoning Rollin to come,
come quickly, come now to help.
Sometime in the night something—
a fox or raccoon—had crossed
that wire and slaughtered the male,
his mangled body a grim
discovery. A grave needed digging.
As she hosed the enclosure
with an aimless thoroughness,
DeDe choked on angry sobs.
The widowed duck stood close by,
still, thinner, tender-aged,
and for once silent.

3

Diamonds of dew in the grass,
smatterings of cherry dark
blood stains, traces of down
like dandelion fuzz dusting
the ground, hose hissing away
all signs of struggle except
the survivor's haunted look
and silence—it all returned
this morning when I saw
a photo of a small boy,
eleven or twelve, grinning
in his camouflage jacket
and matching, flat-brimmed ball cap.
Home from pastureland, he holds
his new waterfowl shotgun
upright against his knee like
a standard. And across his chest
a wreath of nine male mallards,
necks dangling like empty sleeves,
heads still shimmering green.
A great start to the season,
reads the caption. The sky
behind offers no place to hide,
no furthering flight but pride.

Our Lady of the Driveway

Remembering R. J. Foster

> *I cannot pray*
> *to a tub*
> *and she cannot bathe*
> *in her position*
>   "On Route 47"

Not the one you saw years ago
in an upturned bathtub, I found
her this time beside a garage door.
In the chill mist and pre-dawn light,
in front of the ramshackle house
someone is trying to renovate,
a three-foot plaster Virgin—
the twin of yours—stands tall in
her white veil and sky-blue mantle
beside a row of yard waste,
recycling, and rubbish bins.
Her hands are flayed open as if
to welcome or bless. Welcome
to the driveway. Park here in peace.
Bless the Kia you rode in on
and the gasoline that fuels it.
Bless the wheels that grip the road
and hold you safe. Let me protect
your ride against all trespasses
of thieves and vandals and even stray
dogs hellbent on marking your tires.

Coral Oak

Remembering Helene Zychowicz

*"With a storm that brought wind speeds of 130 mph"
253 trees in Point Place "will likely die . . ."*
      The Blade, *4 July 2023*

Of the sea but elevated
in a way I haven't seen since,
a chunk of mushroom coral
as large as a Tuscan loaf
hovered four feet off the ground
in the fork of the oak. Bright white
like swan feathers, it was lodged there
like a molar. Nothing could pry
it loose as long as the tree stood
like a pillar on the hill.

As a child, I ran my fingers
lightly across its bone-stiff ridges.
I marveled at how it became
embedded in the dark gray bark.
According to one story,
my grandmother, who never went
to church but prayed every day
nonetheless, pinched it from a shrine
to the Virgin Mary and set it
beside the oak sapling in her yard.

Seasons passed. The trunk grew, embraced
the coral, and lifted it skywards
like a prayer or an offering.
The oak thrived as if blessed, steadfast

against calamities, its acorns
so plentiful they crunched underfoot.
Can't quite credit the family lore?
That's fine. Her faith was much the same,
unlikely yet so durable only
a tornado could drag it down.

Kepler's Snowflake
Prague, 1611

From out of the murk of darkness above,
flakes of white tumble into sight.
At first he fails to notice, preoccupied.
Crossing *Prožsky most,* his heels
loud on frigid stone and gritty ice,
he pauses halfway across

to admire what little he sees
of the river in winter flood
by the light of the fire beneath
the cross. What to give his patron
friend who frees his mind with funds?
Playful connoisseur of little

nothings who needs nothing but words
of wit to enliven his days.
What nothings could he give for fun?
Not sparks off flint, nor fireflies
of ash popping free from glowing coals,
nor threads of taper smoke, nor strokes

of soft breezes twitching leaves. Not a drop
of water kissing the lip of a jar,
nor a bead of wine on a fingertip,
nor even a speck of dust stamped
on a poppyseed—none of these
is small enough to please.

Cold has numbed his nose. The air heaves.

His eyes tear. Flakes fall briskly now
like stars drifting from a starless sky.
They hook and cling together or
else float individually and light
on his coat sleeve where they linger

for a moment before dissolving.
He admires their form as more touch
wool, each distinctly six-cornered,
six tiny radii tufted like feathers,
no two seemingly the same.
Why six? Why not five or seven?

Then it strikes him: *nix, nichts, nihil.*
With that old, true stirring of joy,
he knows he has found his nothing
and more: sixes galore. He pictures
bees building sturdy honeycombs,
seeds packing the rinds of pomegranates,

hexagonal tiles, stacks of cannonballs,
and more—primroses and white lilies,
pears and apples, cross sections
of cucumbers, saltpetre, rock
crystals, and mysteries of vapor
freezing unseen in the clouds.

As quickly as snowflakes fade,
a universe germinates from
their crystalline moment. He turns
for home to write it all down,
a hen again grubbing for grain
among pebbles, dirt, and dung.

Procrastination

I loathe chores left undone:
moss unchecked on the roof,
fence picket snapped in two,
mound of mulch decaying
in the driveway. I loathe
the bed unmade, towels
unfolded, socks unpaired
in a pile—*un-*, *un-*, *un-*,
too many *uns*—the tub
unscrubbed, plants unwatered,
cracks unspackled above.
A drain too slow to flow,
door hinge hanging loosely,
window frosted with grit.
The more I look, the more
I notice: a silted
wine glass marooned unwashed,
a scatterplot of crumbs
across stove and counter,
dusty book shelves lording
over the dust-bunnyed floor.
I loath the leavings of
chores undone, how they scorch
a morning or a day,
and their collateral
unravelings, how they
undo me feeling me.

The Studio

Even before he died
she lost the will to paint.
Pigments scabbed her palette.
Dust clotted the bristles
of upright brushes in
a jam jar. She had shoved
her desk aside to stack
boxes and bales of straw.
One painting she barely
started: a cloud-streaked sky
above a blank space where
birches or wild flowers
once might have flourished.

Air stagnated for weeks.
Days became migrations
of sunsets and shadows
to the throb of cicadas,
nights, the songs of crickets,
or later, of crackling ice.
One storm four springs ago—
a flash and a gunshot
breakage. A limb stove in
a roof panel, venting
a chute to boughs above.
Leaves blew in. Rain splattered
down in thick rivulets.

Water wetted frames, books,
and shelves of *National*

Geographics, a morgue
of photos lost to rot.
It sluiced through the gash
and pooled where it pointed
on the warped wooden floor.
Twenty or so unframed
watercolors leaning
against one wall softened
and moldered. Black and brown
splotches bloomed in halos
and coronas of white.

Later, when I asked if
she had any paintings
for me, the studio
reeked of straw and mold.
Stacked artwork sagged and sloped.
Paintings stuck together
as if glued. When I tried
to peel one board free,
the suck and rip of colors
shorn hollowed my stomach.
And she stood there watching
as if bearing witness
to someone else's life.

How Much

That poem just now, what did it cost?
Pennies' worth of ink leaked from half
a dozen wells during more months
    than I can recall.

Eleven pages, dense with notes,
scribbles, and cross-outs strewn across
a buffed black Moleskin like so much
    jetliner wreckage.

Five billowing conversations—
three on long walks, two in Irish
pubs—and fifty more with myself
    and the wind and rain.

More: a willingness to dredge what
decades managed to silt and still,
one fearless moment, and the grit
    to see it through.

For you? Much simpler: a minute
or two of your life, the right mood,
and the grace of your attention.
    A bargain for us both.

St. Francis and the Fishes

So when the king of Naples seeks to tempt
the vegan saint, he signals his serving man.

A silver tray of four fried trout is brought
and offered to Francis where he sits. Crisp,

browned, and yellowed, the seared fish smell of oil,
their upstaring eyes as blank as pebbles.

Insouciant, the saint rises from the table
and commands the serving man to follow him.

The king's page tags along. All three go
out to the courtyard where a fountain plumes.

Francis plucks one dead fish by the tail,
lowers it to the deep basin, and lets go.

It plunks in like an ingot. But then burnt
scales slough off, its body curls and softens,

a rainbow of colors infuses its back,
and with a jerk, the trout starts to swim.

Can the serving man hold his tray steady
in the face of this resurrection? Does the fish

begin to stir between the saint's fingertips?
Or must it touch water for the cure to take hold?

Either way, the wide-eyed boy is hooked.
When the swimming fish stops its circling

and lifts its head to gaze at Francis,
the page boy asks, *Can we see that again?*

Daily Rounds

from Cross Street to Kirwan's Lane

For days I chanced upon her traces:
a patch of flakes on a flagstone,
a white line footing stone steps,
a flock of pigeons crowding a wall
as if at a trough. All random

noticings until the moment
I see her in action, an old
woman with ashen hair in
a raven's nest bun, a plum shawl,
and a brisk, migratory gait.

One trailing hand pulls a flimsy
wire cart while the other cradles
a sack of rolled oats. She plunges
in and out of crowds and threads
her way through Latin Quarter streets.

Now and then she stops, sets the cart
upright, and scatters two handfuls
on the ground—always two as if
one can never be enough. No
pattern to her drop zones, at least

none that I can see: the rusted base
of a Bruscar bin, the lowest block
of a quoin, the dingiest cobbles
of an alley way. Whenever
the rolled oats dust the ground,

pigeons swoop from unseen nooks above,
their wingbeats a tippering,
their shadows wild. They swarm and mob
each patch with frenzied jostling like
the flame tips of waves in a storm.

And when some stranger happens by,
they burst into cooing flight
and streak away like meteors
across the sunshine and shadows
of an otherwise weary afternoon.

Carpenter's Square

From papa's hands to mine and who knows where before it came to me like a measurer's tomahawk, full of ceremony and use. I seldom know exactly where it is but always manage to find it. Its foot-long rule, as stiff and sharp-cornered as an unhammered blade has browned over time. Oil spots like liver spots darken the four, ten and eleven and rust is lichen-bright in the groove where the blue angling grip holds the rule fast, square and true. I place its right angle against the long side of a board, bridge two measured marks and drag the carved pencil tip along the straight edge—sure my line will guide the saw. Then, afterwards, the same right angle decides how well hand and handsaw stayed square and true. Another board, another hand-drawn line, the square sighting my way until the job is done. One's love for a tool is occasional, the stuff of here and now, based on mutual, momentary need, then forgotten until the next need comes along. But the square's love for work is pure. After the last *cut* is made, and the board end falls away, after the last screw is driven home, and the last of the sawdust swept up, it rejoins the other tools on my crowded bench where, in darkness, it dreams of all the unmade lines on all the unmarked boards in all the years to come.

Tempting the Undertow

Blue-shirted, the boy has waded
chest-high into rollers roaring
like waterfalls after a storm.

His lips faint bruises, his calves gone numb,
he hops around as much for warmth
as out of fear of falling under,

his knees long past pins and needles,
his hands as wrinkled as walnut shells.
Each wave brings a shudder.

Each wave rides the slow rise of sand
and surges higher than his head,
then shrugs and breaks into block-long

white caps and tumbles right at him
like an avalanche. Boiling foam
threatens him with the undertow.

Yet he stays rooted. He stares it down
until the onrush almost strikes.
Then he runs with great loping strides

toward shore and all he's learned so far.

Circuit

for Tyler and Sam on their wedding day

Your work to-date has been meticulous.
All the outlets are where you need them,
all the fixtures too. You threaded cable through
the walls of your every day, plated each

joist and stud, and left enough play for life's
accidents, those nails that go astray
without a thought of what's beneath. No bad
splice, no loose wire will break its sheath.

Sure, there'll be brownout and blackout days
when the power cuts off, and all the light
seems squeezed from your home as if from a sponge.
But these won't last past a candle's lifespan.

Your current is strong, your breakers infallible.
Your years together ground this circuit.
No storm, no surge, no overload now
will fry the wiring or cause it to fail.

Five Friends

As if in answer to an unknown prayer,
five wooden figures dance beyond the trunks
of cherry trees—unmissable in the morning
drop-off rush, headless, handless, footless,
yet somehow children nonetheless.

Their arms undulate like waves on deep
water, their trek a push-me-pull-you
toward Saghalie's front door. Any one of them
could be any child on a different day.
The two in front, knees bent, keenly intent

on beating first bell, strain to haul the others
onward. The next two, game for whatever
comes along, lampoon their strident strides.
The last angles for escape, the day too steep
to climb. He keeps the line from being straight.

In summer glare, they point the way to new
beginnings. In winter dark, they ghost
wind and sleet. In spring mizzle, they blush
under drifting clouds. Yet always the same words:
five Chinese characters in a bendy verse, saying

person, person, person, person, person,
monolithic *yes* to all doubters passing by.
Five friends, they must be, together unafraid
to let loose their sparrows of laughter
or hold on tightly if ever one starts to fall.

To Chloe on the Way to Inis Mór

The *Saoirse Na Farraige*, same
ferry we rode together two
years ago clears the breakwater
fronting Galway Bay. Cloud cover
mutes the morning and chills the air.

Water mirrors the sky but darkly
like shale or limestone liquified.
Distant sunshine lights a narrow
band of ochre hills in County Clare.
The sky may clear for Dún Dúchathair,

torqued hand of outstretched stone above
the nests of fulmars and razorbills.
Open water now with light chop.
White caps break into stray commas
and dashes but no exclamations.

No CRÍU man patrols the aisles
to offer free refills of striped bags.
Scores of heads above vinyl cushions
sway in unison against each dip
like brown flowers in breaths of wind.

Bow splashes wing past. Some fan
the glass like jets in a car wash.
Hours from now they will dry
into the ghosts of thrown surf,
and I will lean my head back, drowsy

from cliffside exposure, face warm
from real and imagined burn,
and booming, rolling wave crashes
in deep coves will linger in the hum
and churn of the boat speeding home.

A Walk Along the Corrib

i.m. Gerald Dawe

Low tide makes the river glide look faster.
    Five swans swim against the current
near O'Brien's Bridge. They tack across
    with muscular kicks but not much headway.

Water gushes from both walled banks, down
    spillways, over rocks, between stone blocks
where you'd think nothing flowed. Any leisurely
    stroll seldom leaves the waterfall roar for long.

A friend tells me melting polar ice will
    inundate Galway in permanent flood.
Imagine waves cresting the Spanish Arch,
    Quay Street cobblestones and flag-bright storefronts

drowned and fading, schools of silvery fish
    circling before broken windows. Imagine
a kingfisher hovering where strings of lights
    crisscrossed at Christmas. Imagine its dive

and splash and rise near dead pub signs.
    Today, though, this place is as you loved it,
all turbulent torrent and rivered air.
    White flashes of gulls wing past. Fine mist

wafts against naked faces. Walkers
    and runners brave toggling sunshine and squalls.
Three fishermen waist-deep in the Salmon Weir
    ply their craft, flick their rods, flourish lines out.

And another man riding a bicycle pulls
    a spare bike beside him by its handlebars.
Its seat is empty, pedals spinning footless.
    Perhaps he steadies it yet for you.

Endings

One day, without warning, the bulb blew.
What once shone as brightly as a page
near a sunlit window flashed to night.

I missed its warm and warming light. I
flicked all the switches I could find, snapped
breakers back and forth in denial.

Too much depends on filaments too
fine. One spark ends a bulb. One pluck breaks
a treble string. One word, a friendship.

Adagio

A milky sky lets loose the softest
of rains. My casement window cranked
open a crack lets in the soothing sound

but not the damp. Drizzle, deepening,
darkens the red bricks of Garrand Hall.
Shadows spread under shifting clouds.

Birds have gone silent but we seldom do
regardless of the weather. Our noises
waver in as if from underwater.

Pop-pop-pops of nail guns blocks away.
Kling-kling of a trolley rumbling near
and fading. The chapel bell tolls

three o'clock as if new hours bring new
beginnings. Not really. Too many
old friends gone, or gone away. And yet

too much still to say. Rain lightens.
A jet scrapes overhead then whines past.
Another follows minutes later, then

another: crowd after crowd belted
in rows and bound for a dozen
elsewheres. No way for me to follow.

Blush

i.m. Carol Morrison

Pale rose with an almost sweet bite
and tang, so cold it mists the glass
I raise to the sky. The sun lights
a flame above the long, thin stem.

A wine in-between, like the way
you trusted us enough to trade
distinctions of student and teacher
for conversations among friends.

Our moveable feast gathered
round your table or sitting room
where irises bloomed, and talk
went well with white Zinfandel.

You opened the pages of 'Twenties
Paris for me, and how words led
from there to Spain or Michigan
or wherever I needed to go.

You gave me the poem as true
possibility, how to wrestle
words into print, Fitzgerald's
glittering sentences, Lucien Stryk,

and those last lines of Joyce's *Dead*,
how they raised the hairs on my forearms
like the touch of snow on the Shannon.
Years ago some disagreement

over nothing much divided
us. I blush now to wonder why
we buried our friendship so deep
no spade managed to reach it.

Mostly I shun all blushing wines
out of sheer wine snobbery. Today,
for you, I pour this glass to hold,
for once, the light of what we shared.

The Storm

i.m. Judith Scherer Herz, 17 August 2024

Rain seldom graces our dry season.
Grasses turn golden ochre on parched ground.

Tonight, though, out of nowhere, a thunderstorm.
They almost never strike us here. Our rains

are more mizzle and drizzle than torrent
and tempest. But not tonight. Lightning strobes

turbulent clouds. Trailing thunder chases
faster and louder, nearing each strobed flash.

Wind rises. A wall slams into our house.
Gusts blast through the yard. Chimes ring to a frenzy.

Hanging baskets of fuchsia toss and sway
as if rounding Cape Horn. Rain blasts in sheets

along the cutting gale. Something wooden
collapses in darkness out of sight.

What better way than this incongruous storm
to mark this terrible day of your death?

And what better reminder of your bright life
than its aftermath? Half a month of rain

in five hours drowns the ground and freshens the air
with the cool fragrance of undergrowth.

The steady patter softens. The last clap of thunder
rolls down a shallow incline of distance

into silence. What hasn't torn loose
or blown over will grow and bloom again

as you more than anyone would wish.

Discards

Some have yellowed pages, some brand new,
these tomes, anthologies, paperbacks
culled from shelves in lifeless offices.
A purge, not by bonfires *per se* but
by heaps in ninety-five-gallon bins, books
like bricks rubbled by a wrecking ball.

No more Grecian urn or snowy woods,
no more leaves of grass or cold sloe gin.
No Western wind or headlighted moose.
No tempests or dew to send roots rain.
Now *Paradise Lost* is lost again
and Austen, Hemingway, Shakespeare, too.

Readiness is not all anymore,
nor will hands enough set many free.
Roads not taken are the most worthwhile,
yet few find their solitary way.
Who will teach them to speak what they feel,
not what censors deem they ought to say?

To Kristin in a Late May Mood

The chapel bell sounds the hour:
eleven chimes waver and fade.

Young women lounge on two picnic
tables bright on the sun-drenched lawn.

I envision you among them,
basking in an aimless yesterday.

Insects have honeycombed the base
of the log bench they named for you.

Creeping butter cup mobs my shoes.
Ferns and fringe cup flood your marker

and best friend's poem etched in stone.
No one now can read the words without

ducking beneath leaf and limb
or wending around redflower currant.

No groundskeeper tends this grove,
though someone shovels dirt near admin.

offices, scrape of metal on metal.
Am I alone in remembering?

Crimson blooms have budded and burst
from the rhodie engulfing your epitaph.

A breeze freshening half-grown leaves
stirs ten thousand shadows.

If you were here, you would say, *laugh
when you can. Years are short enough.*

A chickadee-dee-dee
lights somewhere on branches above.

Barn Burning

The stench of smoke drew us outside.
A gray plume towering in darkness
beyond the last houses told us
where to go. We hopped a fence,
and there in the flat of stubbled
fields bulldozers had not yet trenched,
the barn burned like a ransacked church.

Silhouettes of neighbors gathered
around as if at a campfire,
but withering heat kept us back.
Flames jetted from hayloft doorways
and higher, slapped the air through holes
in the gabled roof. Sirens lurked
in the distance, circling nearer.

Smoke looked mountainous above.
The fire roared as if fueled by gas
and maybe it was. Where cows
or horses or tractors used to go,
builders had parked back hoes and earth
movers, now engulfed like the rest.
One great tire ruptured with a whump

and sigh. Its Caterpillar sagged
like a steer dropped to one knee.
Our eyes watered, our throats stung.
A downdraft of ash pelted
our faces like a swarm of midges.
Yet we kept watching. No one spoke.
Sirens swelled and filled the field.

Death of an Ohioan

He made nothing with his hands,
not a painting nor a poem,
not a garden nor a greenhouse,
not a single dish from scratch.

He couldn't hang a curtain rod
or mend a wall or fix a tap
or wield a saw with anything
like success. Nor did he try.

He liked to say he was *slightly
to the right of Atilla the Hun*,
told hairlip jokes, managed
men, and overspoke women.

His marks were mostly negations,
squiggles through horse histories
on racing forms, Xs nixing
sure losers, crossed out wagers

on lost college football games.
He wrote nothing meant to last,
his doings, the ink on newsprint,
his weeks, empty bottles in bins.

One drunken night a fall crushed
his right pinky, paralyzing
it straight. He let it be. Why grip
anything fully? Or for long.

And when he lost his nerve and job
and friends he made along the way,
and creditors hounded his number
and drove him from state to state,

he shed one name for another,
shed heirlooms, photos, and reminders.
He made nothing with his hands
and held nothing but his last breath.

Back Through Snoqualmie Pass

Inauguration Day, 2025

Elsewhere politicians gather to swear
in the most corrupt of men. They hide
indoors from the crowds and cold. No flags
half-staffed, no mourners allowed. Fires scour
California hills. Bluffs crumble. Homes topple
into the sea. The wronged stay wronged and weaken.
Sewage kills rivers, soil chalks into dust,
algae blooms, and millions die, glassy-eyed.

Oh, Tao Yuanming, old friend from afar,
how well you knew the venom of the rich
and their bone-deep itch for more. We cross
the summit near sunset, our ears stoppered
against the charlatan's nasally rants.
Cliffs along the highway weep falls of ice.
Firs in snow abide. Teach me to find my plot
of peace. This time I promise to listen.

Street Moment

He camps in front of Hodges Figgis
facing the doorway and all who pass
like a chieftain seated to parlay,
his docker's cap a fire pit for his cup.

*Will that tourist with his chemist's bag
danglin' from his hand spare me a glance
or coin?*
            No help for it but to try:
spare some change mister rasps out like
the bright edge of a shovel across concrete.

The Squirrel

No longer see-sawing leaps
across dead grass, it shambles

up two steps to our back porch
like a shipwreck survivor.

It stops, stalls, seems to lose
its bearings, then sniffs the air

as if scents alone can still
the drunken vertigo no

rest will cure. It totters,
leans, lists to the left, then rights

itself as best it can, and
finally reaches my out-

stretched hand to pluck a peanut
from my fingers. Then back, back,

back again the way it came,
its slow crawl full of pauses.

It stops once more in a patch
of shade to crack open the shell

aaaaand . . . topples over—but doesn't
let go. It knows nothing but

that nut it cherishes with
mouth, teeth, and tongue. It will keep

burying nuts in shallow
ground it forgets more fully

each passing day. Soon, a week
perhaps, the yard will forget

it lived here. The jays won't miss
its competition. And later squirrels

won't know unless round worms
devour *their* worlds from inside out.

The Abscessed Lover

A kettle lid of clouds
purples a sunset
arrived too soon.
What lights him like
a beacon fire: the smile

in her voice when she says
his name—her voice he fears
he barely remembers.
And now another season
passes without any

prospect of her. He drinks
another mouthful of ale
tasting of pine needles
and second guesses.
Words he imagines speaking

but never will gust
the treetops of sleepless nights.
Each fragrant slow burn
of days leaves nothing more
than a broken trail of ash.

Fear

Sleep's assassin, twisted sheet, shallowed breath,
worrier of muscles, stoker of sighs,
heartbeat's avalanche, ache-tormented eyes,
rope-tied diaphragm, unripe fig of death.

Psalter of stale hurts, rage held close and kept,
rock through a window, effigy on fire,
firestorm of blame and billionaires' desire,
vomit of lies the worst of us accept.

A scythe, a shiv, a wound past all prevention,
a toxin of guilt, pungent and bold;
the broken glass of best intentions,
jagged and hard and splintery and cold—

permafrost of grief, bud that never thrived,
storm of lost chances, child within buried alive.

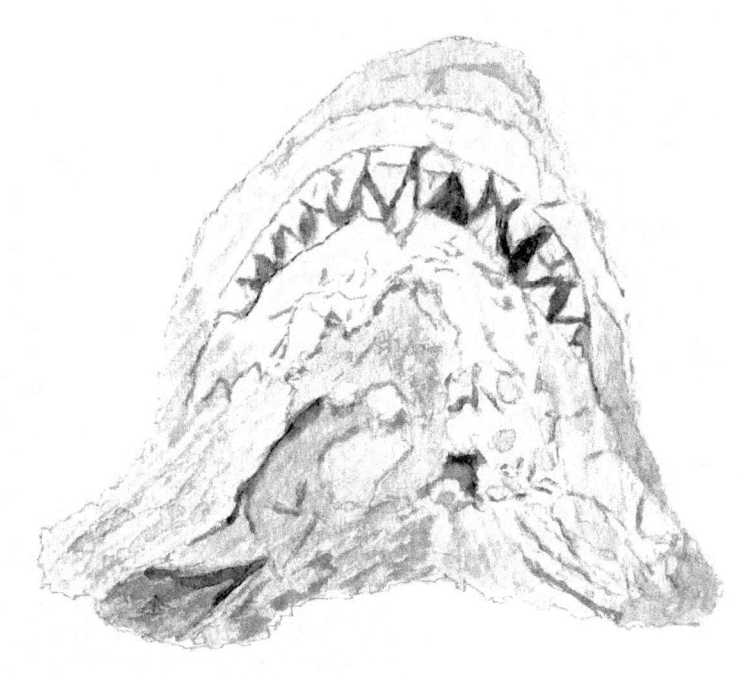

Glossopetrae

Florence, 1667

They hacked off the head of the monster we
know as *carcharodon carcharias*,
the great white shark, and carted it fast
to Florence. Its carcass they cast in the sea.

Its stench on Steno's table twisted guts
and watered eyes. Yet the grand duke, his brother,
and their hangers-on crowded round to stare
at the huge, blunt head and eyes still moist.

Steno's scalpel sliced tough skin and muscle.
His deft fingers splayed open cuts in tender
flesh, plucked tendons, and peeled layer by layer
as if guided more by touch than sight. A tussle

with cartilage split apart what passed for skull
and therein a parsnip brain with dangled
double sprouts. What were these for? And how could
such small bundles steer the skiff-sized tail

now cast away? Steno and his helpers
flipped over the slab of a head. Its jaw
hung slack, a maw studded with arrow
tips and large enough to gulp a man in armor.

Onlookers gasped. The bishop crossed himself.
Steno wondered not at God but at the shape
of those teeth, thirteen rows, some barely lipped
from gum. Opportunists along the way had helped

themselves to the choicest of the outermost,
disturbing the line with gaps in the grisly
grin like notches in the blade of a saw. Simile
sailed his imagination to the coast

of Malta, where shell and tongue stones strewed
the rocky ground after hard showers. Tongue stones—
those pointed curiosities, poison
antidotes, wards against a sorcerer's

spells, remedies for fever and falling sickness,
charms to court young women, ease the agony
of childbirth, or loosen the speech of the tongue-tied.
No wonder the Maltese sold them by the gross.

He bloodied his forceps in wrenching a tooth free,
laid it beside its tongue stone twin, and saw then
sure proof of sediments turned mountains,
shale silting shells, and whispers of ancient seas.

St. Francis and the Strait of Messina

This day when sunlight glitters on the strait,
and the salt-tinged air smells fresh, not rotten,
all Francis desires is peace enough
to found a hermitage of Minims
among the wine makers and olive groves
on the rolling hills of Sicily.

What can be simpler? Take a ship over,
talk with people, enjoy the journey, and walk
to where God or impulse guides him. Then let
seed and sprout whatever will take root.
He waits to board the caravel, Brother
Adopho restless and shuffling behind him.

But when they come to climb the gangplank,
the head boatman surveys their worn
woolen cloaks and thrice-mended habits,
their dingy rope belts and grimy bare feet,
shakes his grizzled, graying head and says,
Not a florin to your names, I suppose.

We are the least of all the faithful,
Francis replies as mildly as he can.
Charity won't buy bread, says the boatman.
Or wine to go with it, adds his fellow.
Both laugh as do passengers in earshot.
Move along. What else can they do?

The friars step out of line. Francis rolls his eyes
toward the billowing clusters of clouds. He sniffs
the air, hears the calls of terns in curling
flight and the low sounds of water lapping,
and descends the stepping stones to the sea.
When splashes touch his toes, he whips

his cloak from off his shoulders, hooks its neck
on his staff, and steps out onto the water.
His cloak holds watertight beneath his feet.
We're going, he says. Adolpho, muttering prayers,
slides on behind him. The cloak fills like a sail,
and off they go, riding the wind and leaving no wake.

Mold-O-Rama

The Field Museum on Saturday,
clamor of crowds wherever I go.
All I have time for are fossils.
They thrilled me as a child.
Pteranodons suspended in
an endless glide, titanosaur
stretching its impossible neck,
mammoth forklifting its tusks.

A guided tour of mass extinctions
spills into a Jurassic hall,
staged scenes of skeletons and what
traces the long-dead dinosaurs
left in stone. I look up from a fossilized
footprint, and there by the doors
to the T-Rex Sue, a different ghost
calls me over—a Mold-O-Rama,

jukebox of magic—and forty-five years
vanish in the rainbow glow of its name.
A glass dome exposes its workings.
The pay slot sucks in my five-dollar
bill, and Mold-O-Rama rumbles awake,
rattles and clacks, revs and hums
like it wants to fly. Two arms
piston together—*namaste*—

a hiss of pressure and plastic. The mold
splits and—surprise!—there it stands,
a shiny red T-Rex, hot from its making.
When I fish it, fragrant, from the drop
chute, I fear I'll leave fingerprints.
Ten-year-olds shout and laugh, voices
echoing in the vaulted hall,
and I am one of them again.

An Anniversary

i.m. Frank Lofendo

Not when I teach my son to tie a tie
for the second or third time, the reverse
angle so tricky I do what you did:
tie it on myself first, then slip the knot
and noose over my head and onto his;

nor when I switchback the growling mower
in neat rows across our fugitive patch
of grass, its dull roar haranguing my ears,
my forearms flecked with grit and bits of green;
nor when I swing your hammer at penny

nails, two taps to seat each one, then a strike
to drive it flush, each tap and blow landing
more by feel than sight; nor when I rewire
an outlet or mend a picket or pinch
a pear for ripeness do I miss you most,

but when I crush and mince garlic cloves
with your meaty carving knife on my bamboo board.
Five years gone today. How can it be?
Yet something of your energy remains
in the handle of the knife I clean and dry,

in the fingerling glass of cabernet
I sip as I cook, and in the garlic
sizzling in oil, how its aroma
rises from the skillet and holds me
and everyone nearby in its embrace.

Fresh-Picked

Not bloated and flavorless
like store-bought blueberries,
these slip petitely off fine stems,
more cloudy sky than blackened bruise.
Around the tongue, they explode
in sweetness the way love does:
forever fresh, forever new.

Boiling Penne

for Kieran and Jensen

Details matter, boys, starting with the pot
and how full you choose to fill it. One too
small will boil over, a cataclysm
of spillage and sizzling, but one too large—

that stock pot, for instance—will test your patience
beyond endurance. Your water must be
clean and cold, fresh from the tap, and no more
than two-thirds high. Now add a little salt,

measured not with a spoon but with your cupped
palm the way your great grandmother used to
because the best flavor starts with feel,
not overthinking. Wishing alone won't cause

water to boil faster. If you hover, time
will bead. Save that gift for your first kiss
or the last summer night you spend laughing
among friends. Cover the pot and do something

else—but don't stray far. You can't know all
you miss when you turn away. Listen, listen
for a slow ticking like the start of rain.
It will swell to a steady whoosh like air

released from a valve or tire. Don't fear
the steam rattling and jetting from where
the lid is loosest. Heat always follows
the rules. Know these and never be afraid.

Now slide in the penne slowly to dodge
the sting of stray drops and splashes.
Water will cloud and grumble. Foam will rise
toward overflowing. Never shrink from threats.

As for time, remember: perfect might be
a minute more or less than expert opinion.
Not every day is *al dente*. Learn to trust
the guidance of what you feel and know.

Then pick your moment. Seize it when it comes.
Set your strainer just so, grip the pot
with both hands, and pour, pour through
the billowing steam, pour like you can't miss.

Painting the Moon

Galileo in Padua, December 1609

The moon looms into view.
    He swivels his glass
to catch one quarter with
    every steady pass.

No smooth, polished sphere
    the way some ancients
taught but chasmed and crabbed,
    blunt and protuberant,

valleyed and peaked and full
    of sinuosities
along the curve that bounds
    its luminosity.

He reaches for paper,
    bistre, brush on hand
to render what he sees
    as quickly as he can.

Dips his brush in water,
    flicks the excess free,
swirls the tip in pigment,
    the soot of beechwood trees.

A brushful of water,
    drained against the lip,
makes a light brown wash that fills
    his miniver tip.

He dabs in spots and knobs
    along the crescent line
as if his hand were shaken
    by red unwatered wine.

Stains of shade rouge the light,
    dimpled crater marks.
Layered shadows darken;
    light squibs jag the dark.

Soon enough he finishes
    hemming the bright arc,
the crescent side complete,
    bordered now and stark.

This moon now joins the others,
    six views to a page.
Which are worth engraving?
    He alone will gauge.

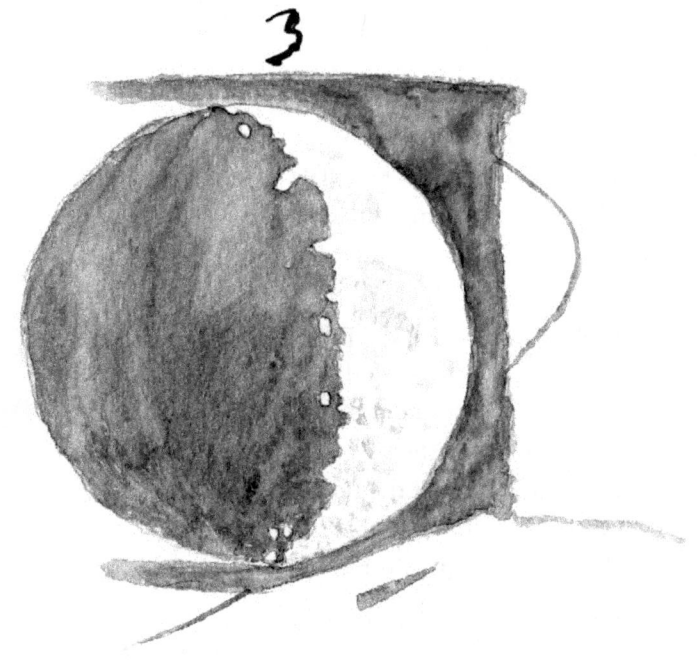

Candle

for Jerry Willins

     A
    tiny
   fla me

sparks from the packed grit
of the match head, touches
the wick. It catches and
widens to a glow warming
morning twilight. The pupil
of wax begins to tear. Hush
as still as forest undergrowth
or unspoken wishes. In your
extremity, against the body's
betrayals and the doubts
they spark on the flint of
sleepless nights, I light
this prayer for you, this
firefly of peace, this moonlit
dew drop of hope, this trickle
of birdsong beckoning dawn.

Undo List

Whatever you do, plan no plans.
Burn your cluttered lists. Slap the hand
that would write more. Dig a hole,
drop in your phone, and plant a tree.
Blame any ringing you may hear
on crickets or frogs, kinglets or
juncos, or the tinkling rain.

Shutter your socials, nullify
your notifications. Reset
your passwords, blindfolded,
your keyboard upside down. Open
each day like an origami
flower delivered by the wind
or a darting hummingbird.

Windchimes are fantastic. They say
nothing more than they must. So are
lakes and rivers and waterfalls, all
great tutors on change and flow. Find
a stream of clear, running water,
rinse your ears of clotting dust, and
let its cold sting your cheeks to life.

Oceans offer free lessons in
forgetting. Learn every one,
barefoot in the sand. Forests, too.
Venture deep among cedars where
sunshine can't bake the soil,
and moisture lingers to nourish
everything it can, including you.

Or if you can't roam so far
afield, undo where you are. Sit
in some quiet place. Close your eyes,
hang your chin on a thread of sky,
and let your breathing calm your heart.
Every life happens one breath
at a time. Free yourself with yours.

New Listing

A lit. professor, slightly used yet still
intact. First edition (believe it or not),
published in 1969. Cloth, of course.
Not ex-library, though libraries often feel
like home. But so do forests, rolling hillsides,
and anywhere in view of open sea
and running water, with scents of lilac,
evergreen, or salt spray hovering near.

Was there ever a dust jacket? If so,
it vanished long ago. The book has braved
a score of shelves without one. Years have sunned
the spine but it remains unbroken,
despite callous treatment from time to time.
The binding, still strong, has eased enough
to lie open where you please. Some edgewear,
yes, but no tobacco smell, no nicks or tears,

creases or dog-earring, misprints or missing leaves.
No previous owner who cannot be forgotten.
The text shines brightly, and the pages are clean
enough—no foxing, no soiling, no marginalia
that cannot be erased—and every now and then
it smells like it was printed yesterday.
Very good on what it has to say. Used,
sure, but rightly seasoned. For you, like new.

www.ingramcontent.com/pod-product-compliance
Lightning Source LLC
Chambersburg PA
CBHW071728040426
42446CB00011B/2272